BASIC CARD MAGIC

25 EASY CARD MAGIC TRICKS FOR BEGINNERS

SAM FURY

Illustrated by
NEIL GERMIO

WARNINGS AND DISCLAIMERS

The information in this publication is made public for reference only.

Neither the author, publisher, nor anyone else involved in the production of this publication is responsible for how the reader uses the information or the result of his/her actions.

CONTENTS

COLOR CHANGES

COLOR CHANGES

THANKS FOR YOUR PURCHASE

Did you know you can get FREE chapters of any SF Nonfiction Book you want?

https://offers.SFNonfictionBooks.com/Free-Chapters

You will also be among the first to know of FREE review copies, discount offers, bonus content, and more.

Go to:

https://offers.SFNonfictionBooks.com/Free-Chapters

Thanks again for your support.

INTRODUCTION

This card magic book has 25 no-setup and gimmick-free card tricks. This means you will be to pick up any standard deck of cards, have your spectator shuffle them, then perform any of the tricks in this book.

This book is split into six sections, and is laid out so you learn a variety of card-magic skills in a progressive manner. If you are a total beginner, start from the start and practice each new technique as you come to it.

If you already know some basic skills, you can skip to any trick you want to learn. If there is a new skill you don't know, use the internal links (if your device allows you to do so) or refer to the contents page to find the tutorial on how to do it.

Each section will teach you fundamental card-magic skills and several tricks to go with them.

In most of the sections, the tricks are combined into a themed sequence. You can use the sequences as they are, tweak them, combine them, mix them up, or use any trick on its own.

Here is a brief explanation of the six sections:

- **Basic Handling**. Basic card handling skills accompanied with "self-working" prediction tricks.
- **Keeping Track**. Several tricks designed to fool your spectator about where his card is.
- **Soulmates**. Soulmates are two cards that share the same face value and color, for example, the ace of hearts and the ace of diamonds. The tricks in this section revolve around this concept.
- **Reversals**. Tricks in which the selected card reveals itself facing in the opposite direction to the rest of the cards.
- **Ambitious Card**. A famous card sequence in which the

spectator's selection continuously returns back to the top of the deck.

- **Color changes**. Several ways to make cards instantly change from one to another, or disappear completely.

TERMINOLOGY

Here is a list of card-magic-specific terminology used in this book:

- **Break**. Creating a gap between the cards that your spectator can't see. Usually done with either your pinky or thumb.
- **Color change**. Instantly changing one card for another.
- **Control**. Moving a card to a certain position in the deck without your spectator knowing.
- **Cut or cutting the cards**. Taking a portion of cards off the top of the deck.
- **Swing cut**. A type of cut where the top packet of cards pivots on your thumb while being transferred to your other hand.
- **Deck**. A full packet of cards.
- **Dominant hand**. The hand you are most comfortable using for common acts, such as writing.
- **Non-dominant hand**. The hand that isn't your dominant hand.
- **Double lift**. Lifting two cards as one.
- **Trick**. A single effect in a sequence.
- **False shuffle**. Shuffling the cards while keeping some or all of them in order.
- **Finishing clean**. Finishing a trick with no evidence of how you did it.
- **Flashing**. Unintentionally showing a card or technique.
- **Flush**. Making or having the cards align perfectly.
- **Force**. Making your spectator choose the card you want her to choose.
- **Force card**. The card you are forcing.
- **Gimmick**. A prop used to make a trick possible that the spectator is unaware of.
- **In-jog**. When one or more cards stick in towards you more than the rest of the packet.

- **Out-jog**. When one or more cards stick out towards you more than the rest of the packet.
- **Method**. How you perform a trick.
- **Packet**. A portion of cards.
- **Patter**. What you say while performing a trick.
- **Peek**. Secretly looking at the value of a card.
- **Picture cards**. Cards that are not assigned a number (such as the jack, queen, and king).
- **Reveal**. The part of a trick that shows that something "magical" has happened.
- **Riffle**. Allowing the cards to leave the grip of your fingers or thumb one by one.
- **Selection**. The card you or your spectator chooses.
- **Sequence**. A number of tricks performed one after another.
- **Setup**. An action you need to do before performing a trick in order to make the trick work.
- **Shuffle**. Mixing up the cards.
- **Sleight**. A technique used to help make the trick work.
- **Soulmates**. Two cards that share the same face value and color.
- **Spectator**. The person for whom you are performing the trick.
- **Squaring**. The act of aligning a packet or deck of cards flush with each other.

BASIC PRINCIPLES OF MAGIC

Here are some fundamental principles which will help you in all areas of magic.

Not all of these principles will apply to every trick, but in general, adhering to them will make your sleights, tricks, and sequences better.

Misdirection

Misdirection is when you draw your spectator's attention to one thing to prevent him from noticing another.

There are two basic ways to do this. The first encourages the spectator to look away. Some examples of this are to:

- Look up, so the spectator follows your eyes.
- Ask him to look at and memorize his card.
- Use patter, so he looks at you instead of your hands.

The second method of redirection is to use a larger movement to cover the smaller one. The idea of this is that the spectator will think the larger movement contains the secret, and so will not pay attention to how the real sleight is happening. A basic example of this is to do a sleight under the guise of squaring up a deck of cards.

Same Actions

Use the same action when doing a sleight as you would when doing the action normally. If you use one action to do something and then another when doing a sleight, it will look suspicious.

Patter

Patter is what you say throughout a trick and/or sequence of tricks. It has several uses:

- **Misdirection.** Engaging patter can distract your spectator from things you don't want him to see.
- **Memory aid.** Creating a story will help you remember the sequence of sleights in a trick and/or the order of tricks in your sequence.
- **Flow.** Jumping from one trick to another without a story to connect them can be awkward. Using patter will help things move along smoothly.
- **Gives a reason.** Sometimes you need to do a certain action to make a trick work, but doing so without a reason would look out of place. Use patter to fill that void.
- **Entertainment.** Having an engaging story to go with your tricks adds entertainment value. Adapting your patter to your personality will help with this as well.

A Light Touch

Learning the sleights needed for close-up magic can be challenging to begin with. You may need to build up dexterity to achieve certain movements.

A common mistake people make while doing this is being too rigid or gripping too hard. When you are having trouble with a certain technique, try using a lighter touch.

As you get better, aim to make your finger movements as slight as possible and fix things that look awkward or out of place.

Angles

For visual sleights, such as color changes and vanishes, angles become increasingly important.

Consider carefully how you position your hands and body in relation to your spectator's line of sight. Using a mirror and/or recording yourself on video can help you pinpoint the best angles to use.

Tapping the Wand

Tapping the wand is a metaphor for having a reason for the "magic" to happen, such as tapping the object with a wand. Without this type of gesture, your reveal has less impact, and in some cases, the spectator may not even realize something magical happened.

There are many ways to "tap the wand," limited only to your imagination. Here are some examples that either you or your spectator can do:

- Tap the object with your pen or a finger.
- Snap your fingers.
- Wave your hand over the object.
- Shout a direction, such as "Rise," at the object.
- Hit down on the object with your hand.

Keeping it Magical

When a spectator sees a well-performed trick for the first time, he gets a sense of amazement. But as soon as he discovers how you did it, the amazement of that trick, and all the following ones, dissipates. This is why you should never reveal your secrets to your spectator.

Besides not actually revealing your methods, here are some tips on how to keep your tricks secret:

- **Don't show the same trick twice.** The first time you show someone a trick, they have no idea what is going to happen. The second time, they will know what to expect and will be looking for how it works.
- **Don't use the same technique too often.** The more

times a spectator sees a specific sleight, the more likely he is to figure out how you did it. Learn several ways to achieve the same result and interchange them throughout your sequence.

- **Practice a lot before performing**. Except for the most basic tricks, you need to practice any single trick at least 10 times before you can try performing it, or your spectator is likely to catch the method.
- **Downplay mistakes**. Mistakes happen. You may drop something, lose his card, or flash your technique. Don't make a big deal about it, and your spectator won't either. You can make a joke about it, or otherwise incorporate it into your patter so the spectator thinks it is part of the performance. Alternatively, just acknowledge it and move on.

BASIC CARD-HANDLING

Learn basic card-handling skills and a prediction-themed sequence with four easy tricks.

GRIPS

Proper card-handling makes performing sleights easier, and it all starts with the correct grip. Here are a few basic grips that are used in this book. Some tricks will use variations of them.

Mechanic's Grip

The mechanic's grip is the standard "go-to" grip for dealing, spreading, counting, and other common techniques. It is comfortable and secure.

Hold the cards in your hand, with your middle, ring, and pinky fingers on the side. Your index finger holds the cards in place diagonally along the front. Your thumb rests on top or along the side and, among other things, can move back and forth to slide cards off the top.

Straddle Grip

From the mechanic's grip, move your pinky finger to the bottom edge of the cards. Hold the cards in place at the edges with the sides of your fingers. When you hold the cards upside down, there will be a gap between the cards and your palm.

Use a deep or shallow grip depending on what you need.

A variation of the straddle grip is the vertical straddle grip. Place your ring and middle fingers on the short edge of the cards with your thumb along the opposite short edge. Your index finger should be on one long side and your pinky finger on the other.

Biddle Grip

Hold the cards in a straddle grip, then move all four fingers to the top edge, so there are no fingers on the longer sides.

A variation of this is to use only your index finger and thumb to hold the cards.

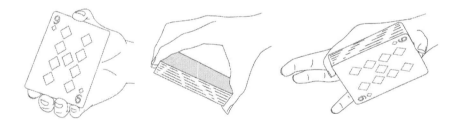

SQUARING THE DECK

After almost every technique you use with cards, you will need to square them up again to use the next one. Squaring up cards is also used to cover up sleights of hand.

Hold the messy pile of cards in a loose mechanic's grip.

Bring over your other hand to pick the cards up in a vertical straddle grip. This will align them a little vertically. Place them back down into your mechanic's grip.

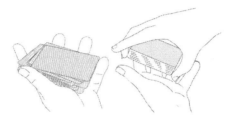

Lightly squeeze the long edges together with your mechanic's grip, so the cards become flush along your thumb.

Slide the thumb and fingers of your other hand along the short edges to finish off the squaring.

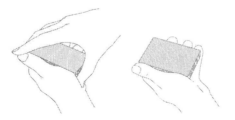

IN-HAND SPREAD

This is a basic spread you can use when asking a spectator to pick a card.

Hold the deck in mechanic's grip in your non-dominant hand. Angle it slightly towards yourself.

Use the tip of your thumb to push a bunch of cards over the tips of your fingers. Bring your dominant hand over to grip the cards between your thumb and the base of your index finger. Your dominant thumb goes on the far side of the top card, in relation to your thumb.

Continue pushing cards with your non-dominant thumb as you extend your dominant hand.

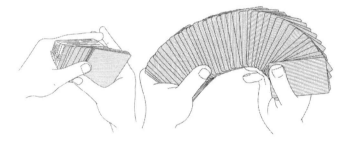

The cards will hold themselves up to a certain point, before they collapse. The better you get, the more you will be able to spread out.

Push the cards back together by closing your dominant hand back on your non-dominant hand, then square the cards up.

OUT-JOGGING

Out-jogging a card is getting it to stick out from the rest of the pack. Amongst other uses, it is a good way for you or your spectator to select one or more cards before actually removing them from the deck. Thumb through the cards as you do an in-hand spread. Have you spectator point to one as you are thumbing through. Use the fingers of your dominant hand, which are underneath the cards, to move the selection up. Hold it in place with your thumb as you move the rest of the cards back down.

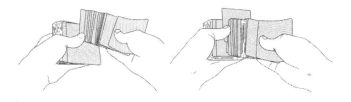

Continue the spread to repeat the process for as many cards as you need. Once all the cards have been selected, bring the spread together so it is a single pile in your non-dominant hand, with all the out jogged cards sticking out the top. Come over with your dominant hand to peel out the out-jogged cards by rotating them over your index finger.

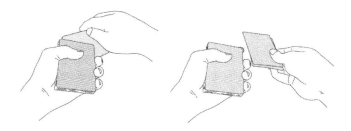

Related Chapters:

- In-Hand Spread

SHUFFLING

Shuffling cards is an important step in many card tricks, because it helps to convince the spectator that his card is getting mixed into the deck.

Shuffling can also be a way to control cards. Doing this is called a false shuffle.

You will learn a couple of false shuffles in this book, but first you need to know the basic shuffling techniques.

It is important that your real shuffle and your false shuffle look the same, so your spectator won't have reason to suspect anything.

There are many ways to shuffle (and false shuffle), but it's best to keep things simple. Here are two common ways to shuffle cards.

Overhand Shuffle

Start with the cards in a mechanic's grip in your non-dominant hand.

Bring your dominant hand over to pinch the short edges. Your thumb should be on one edge and your middle, ring, and pinky fingers on the other. Curl your index finger on the back of the cards.

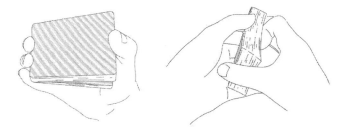

Use the thumb of your non-dominant hand to grab a small number of cards (around ten is good), while using your dominant hand to lift the rest of the packet up.

Bring the pack in your dominant hand in front of the cards in your non-dominant hand, so your thumb can slide off more cards.

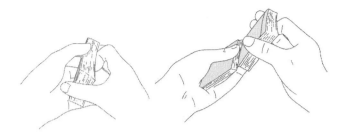

Repeat this movement. Each time you slide cards off, they should land on top of the ones already in your non-dominant hand.

Continue to do this until there are no cards left in your dominant hand. You can just drop the last cards on top.

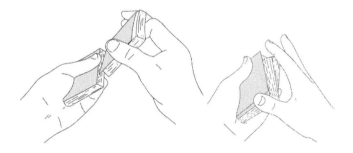

You can repeat this process as much as you want. When you're finished, square up the deck.

Riffle Shuffle

Start with the about half the deck in each hand, in vertical straddle grips. The faces of the cards in both hands should be facing each other.

The cards should be near the tips of your thumbs and at about the first joint of your other fingers. Move the cards deeper into your fingers, but closer to the tips of your thumbs.

Curl your index finger into the middle of the cards and use it to apply opposing pressure as you pull back with your thumb and fingers.

Bring the thumb edges of the two piles together and gradually slide your thumbs back along the top edges, allowing the cards to riffle through into each other so they overlap.

Make sure you keep the base of the cards low and get a good bend. If you angle the cards too high and/or don't get close enough to a 90-degree bend, they won't fall properly.

From here, you can square the cards together, or go into the bridge.

To do the bridge, place your thumbs on top to hold the cards in place.

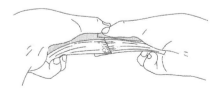

Push and bend the cards in the bridge up into an arch then gradually release the pressure at the bottom of the bridge to allow the cards to fall.

Square up the deck to finish.

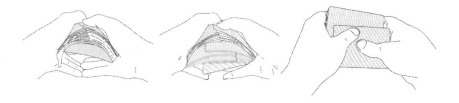

Doing the riffle shuffle slowly may damage the cards if you hold them in a bent position for too long, but doing it quickly will have almost no effect on them.

Related Chapters:

- Grips

FALSE SHUFFLES

A false shuffle is when it appears that you're shuffling normally, but in reality you're keeping some or all of the cards in the same order. It is a fundamental skill you can use at any time you need to in order to convince your spectator nothing funny is going on.

False Overhand

The false overhand will keep all the cards in the exact same order. From the spectator's point of view, it looks identical to the normal overhand shuffle explained earlier in this book.

If you use a normal overhand shuffle and this false shuffle in the same sequence, ensure the tempo of your shuffles match, or you may raise suspicion.

The hand positions and actions for the false overhand are almost identical to the normal overhand shuffle.

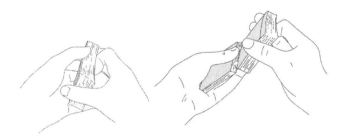

The difference is that you place the stripped cards behind your curled finger.

The next cards you strip go behind the cards behind your curled finger, and so on.

At the end, toss all the cards on top of the remaining packet.

Keep a steady rhythm so it looks natural.

False Riffle Shuffle

This false shuffle is good for keeping the top and/or bottom several cards in the same place. For most of the tricks in this book, this is all you need.

You could just do the false overhand, but unless you need all the cards in the same order, it's a good idea to follow up with the false riffle shuffle. This will really convince your spectator that the chosen card is mixed into the deck.

The false riffle shuffle is exactly the same as a normal riffle shuffle. Just make sure that the chosen card(s) lands on the top or bottom of the deck, as needed for the trick you are performing.

Related Chapters:

- Shuffling

RIBBON SPREAD

A ribbon spread is when you slide out the cards on a table to display them for your spectator. It works best with a newer pack of cards and on a surface that is not too slippery.

Hold the deck in a vertical straddle grip, but with your index finger along the side. Place the cards on the surface on the opposite side of the hand you're holding them with.

Use steady pressure with your index finger on top of the cards as you slide your hand across the table to fan the cards out.

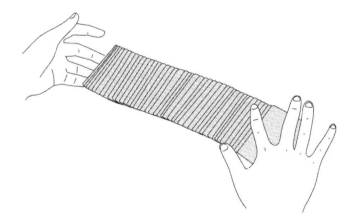

To flip the cards, lift up the first few cards with your finger and then push them over. Do it with a bit of force, but not too much.

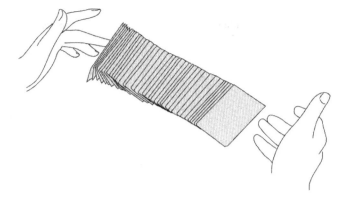

Catch the last cards that flip over with your index and middle finger on the other side and flip them back the other way. You can do this back and forth.

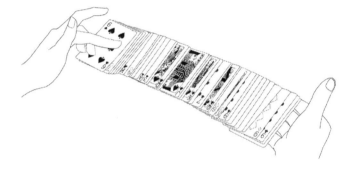

When you're ready, scoop up the cards and square them off in your hand.

You can do the ribbon spread in different directions and shapes. This will make flipping and/or scooping them up harder, or even impossible, depending on the shape.

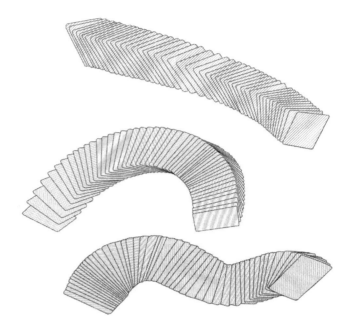

PREDICTION SEQUENCE

The theme for this sequence revolves around prediction. In the first two tricks, the cards help with some clever counting to find your spectator's selected card. In the last two tricks, you predict what choices he will make.

MAGICAL NINE

Your spectator chooses any nine cards, and from those, one becomes his selection. The selection is mixed into the nine cards, and then the value of his selection is spelled out with the nine cards. The last card is his selection.

Method

Shuffle the deck and have your spectator do the same.

Use the in-hand spread to fan the cards out and ask him to pick any nine cards. Put the remainder of the cards aside. Place the nine cards on the table in three piles of three cards each.

Ask the spectator to choose any pile and flip it over. Whichever card is showing on the top of the now face-up pile is his selection.

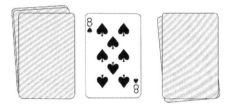

Join the two face-down packets together and shuffle them. Pick up the last pile and place it face down on top of the other two packets. Now his card is in the third position from the top. Don't show this to the spectator.

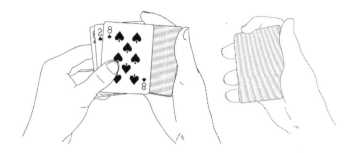

Tell the spectator that when you click your fingers over the deck (or do whatever gesture you prefer), the card will magically move to the right position in the pile. This is a bit cryptic, but once you perform the trick, the spectator will get it.

Spell the first word of the value of his card as you place down each card—one letter for each card. For example, if his card is the eight of spades, you will be placing down five cards, each one on top of the previous one.

E - I - G - H - T

At the end of the word, place the rest of the cards directly on top.

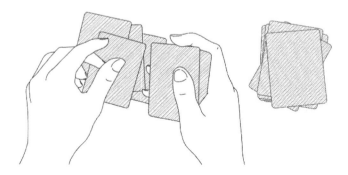

Pick up all the cards and spell out the next word.

. . .

O - F

Do it again.

S - P - A - D - E - S

Finally, do it with the magic word "MAGIC," or any other five letter word. For example, if his name is Peter, you can use that.

M - A - G - I - C

As long as you followed the instructions correctly, the card you landed on (the C, if you're using the word "magic") will be his card.

Related Chapters:

- In-Hand Spread

PREDICTION COUNT

The nine cards are mixed back into the rest of the deck. The spectator then chooses four random cards. You place these four cards are placed face up on the table and deal cards on top of each one. You then return the dealt cards to the deck.

You add up the face value of the four cards your spectator chose. You deal that number of cards on the table, magically ending with his selected card.

Method

As you gather up the cards from Magical Nine trick, ensure his card is on top of the nine-card packet. Place the rest of the deck on top. Now his card is ninth from the bottom. Do some fake shuffles, ensuring that his card remains ninth from the bottom.

Right now, the card will be in the 44th position from the top. That is, if you count out 44 cards, the 44th one will be his card.

Tell your spectator that you are now going to predict where his card is in the pack, but you need his help, since the card is connected to him.

Ask him to choose any number below 20. Deal off the number of cards he chooses.

Now it's your turn to pick a number. Choose 24 - the number he chose. For example, if he chose 14, your number will be 10 (24-14=10).

Place the rest of the deck on top of the pile on the table, then pick all the cards up. Ask him to choose another number under 20. Deal that many cards down.

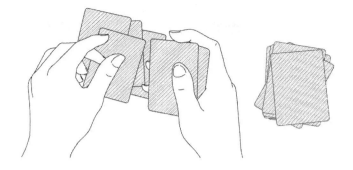

For your number, choose 20 - the number he chose. For example, if he chose 7, your number will be 13 (20-7=13).

The last card you deal down will be his card. If you're using the example above, the 13th card will be his.

Related Chapters:

- Magical Nine

DEAL OR SWITCH

In this trick, all the cards from a single suite are separated from the deck and you explain that you will make predictions about whether your spectator will choose to have you switch or deal them.

You put the cards in the order you predict he will choose. As you place the cards face down on the table, the spectator tells you to either deal or switch the cards. When you flip the cards back over, they are all in order as you predicted.

Method

Using your spectator's card from the previous two tricks, take out all the cards in the same suite. For example, if his card was the eight of spades, take out all of the spade cards. Tell your spectator to put the cards in sequential order as you take them out. That way, he can ensure you get them all.

Put the rest of the deck aside.

Explain to your spectator that you are going to deal the cards on the table according to what he tells you. Show him to demonstrate.

If he tells you to *deal*, place the top card straight down.

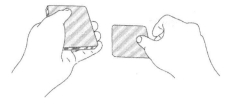

If he tells you to *switch*, take off the top two cards and swap their positions.

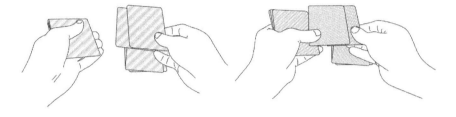

Then place them down.

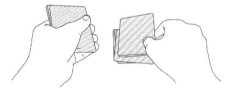

Tell your spectator that you will now make the predictions. Switch the cards around as if you are putting them in a different order, but at the end they must stay in their original sequential order.

While you are switching the cards around, mention to your spectator that you will predict the number of times he will switch, as well as where he will switch. Saying this while you are pretending to mix the cards up will draw his attention away from them.

Ask for "deal or switch," and deal the cards according to what your spectator says, as previously explained. Do this for all the cards, so you are left with one pile on the table. If you are left with one card at the end, just place it on top.

Turn the cards over and fan them out, revealing that you correctly predicted the order he chose. The cards will be reversed, but in sequential order.

This works because whether your spectator says deal or switch, the top card always goes down first, thus keeping the order of the cards correct.

OUT OF THIS WORLD

The spectator shuffles the cards and chooses half of them to use in the trick. From that half, two cards are selected to be "marker" cards: one red and one black.

You put the cards in the order you predict he will choose. As you deal each card, the spectator says whether he thinks it is red or black. After all the cards are dealt, you reveal that you correctly predicted what he would choose.

Method

Tell your spectator that you now have a feel for how his mind works, and can now do a similar prediction with more cards.

Have him shuffle the full deck of cards, cut them into two equal packets, then choose one of the packets.

Take your spectator's chosen pile and start to sort them so that when the cards are faced down, all the red cards are together on top and all the black cards are together on the bottom. Do not let him see.

As you are sorting the cards, tell your spectator that this time you will predict the colors he is going to choose. To make the sort more believable, pause and look into your spectator's eyes as if trying to figure out what he will choose.

Once you are finished sorting, select one red card and one black one. Find a pair if you can, preferably picture cards or aces.

Put the selected red and black cards face up on the table next to each other. These are the indicator cards.

Before you square up the cards, in-jog the top black card. This is so you know when the next color starts. Turn the cards face down. You are ready to deal.

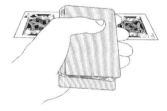

Take off the top card. Do not show it to the spectator. Ask him what color he thinks it is. Whatever color he says the card is (red or black), put it with the corresponding indicator card.

Do this for all the red cards, one at a time.

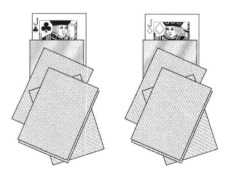

Once you get to your in-jogged card, tell your spectator that you will now make it a bit harder for him by switching the cards around.

Take the red indicator card and put it on top of the black pile. Take the black indicator card and put it on top of the red pile.

Now continue dealing as before, until all the cards are gone.

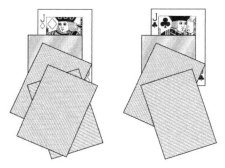

Separate the piles where the indicator cards where. Flip the cards over to reveal that your spectator chose the correct colors.

KEEPING TRACK

Learn four tricks in which your spectator needs to keep track of her card but continuously gets fooled.

To do these tricks, you will learn some fundamental skills such as creating breaks and the double lift.

PEEKING

Peeking is when you take a quick look at a card without your spectator noticing. There are numerous ways to do this. Here are a couple of ideas:

- Try to look at the bottom card while the spectator is shuffling them.
- Square the cards up in your hand while they face towards you to peek at the bottom card.
- Slide out the top card a little before squaring the cards up while they face towards you.
- Spread the cards face up to show the spectator they are all mixed up. You can peek at almost any card using this method.

Related Chapters:

- Shuffling

KEYCARD

The keycard is similar to peeking, but with this technique, you look at the card above or below the spectator's selection. Once you know the keycard, you know your spectator's selection will be directly before or after it.

There are many ways to use the keycard method. Here is a basic one:

Riffle down a deck of cards and ask your spectator to say "stop" whenever she wants. When she does, split the cards into two packets at that point. Allow her to take off the top card of the bottom packet.

Ask your spectator to memorize her card, and then place it back on the top of the bottom packet. As she is looking at the card, peek at the bottom card of the top packet. This is your keycard. Now you know your spectator's card is directly underneath your keycard.

Cut the cards on the table and allow her to cut the cards also. You can also do a couple of false overhand shuffles.

Related Chapters:

- Peeking

BREAKS

A break is when you separate a packet of cards in a way that your spectator doesn't notice.

Pinky Break

To get a pinky break on the top card, push the top card over with your thumb. Use your pinky to push up on the top card and then slide the top card back.

You want the break to be as small as possible so it doesn't show from the spectator's point of view.

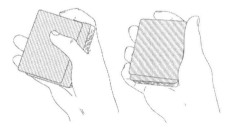

Often, you will need to get a pinky break on more than one card. To do this, riffle up the cards with your thumb until you have the number of cards you need, and then slip your pinky in.

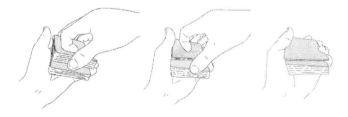

It will help to use some redirection while doing this. You can riffle up the deck a couple of times while talking to the spectator. This is a common thing to do with a deck of cards. On the last time you do it, get the pinky break.

To cover the action, riffle up the back, get the break, then riffle up the front.

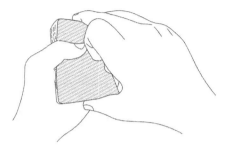

Another way to get a pinky break on multiple cards is to ask your spectator to choose some cards—however many you need. Get a pinky break on the first card and place the additional cards on top.

To get a pinky break on one or more cards on the bottom of the deck, square up the cards and then lightly riffle down the bottom few cards with your pinky until you have the number you need.

Thumb Break

A thumb break is the same concept as a pinky break, but it is held with your thumb. Often, you get a pinky break first and then transfer it to a thumb break.

Assuming you have a pinky break with your dominant hand, come over with your non-dominant hand to grab the deck in a biddle grip. Your thumb should maintain the break between the two piles.

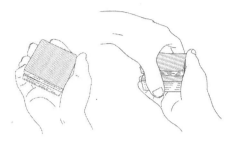

DOUBLE LIFT

A double lift is when you show the spectator one card when there are actually two. It is an essential skill to learn, and features in many tricks.

There are several ways to do the double lift. Here you will learn two basic ones.

Basic Double Lift

To do the basic double lift, you first need to get a pinky break on the top two cards. See the Breaks chapter to learn how to do this.

Once you have the break, ensure the two cards are squared up, then pick them up and show the face value to your spectator.

Applying a little pressure to the back of the two cards with your index finger will ensure they do not split.

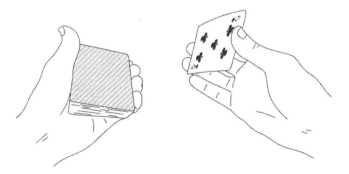

Push-Off Double Lift

This is a little harder to do than the basic double lift, but it looks more natural.

Start with the deck in mechanic's grip.

Use your thumb to apply slight pressure on the top, and straighten your fingers at the same time. The aim is to angle the cards a little.

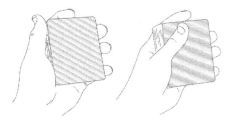

Use your index finger to riffle the cards until you get the top two cards. Place your middle finger in the gap and your thumb on top.

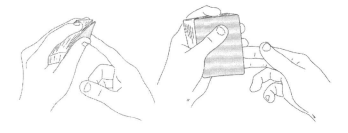

Don't pinch the cards too tightly, or they will separate.

Slide the cards along the top of the deck and flip both of them over.

Sliding them on the deck uses the deck as support to keep them together. Do this casually, with light fingers.

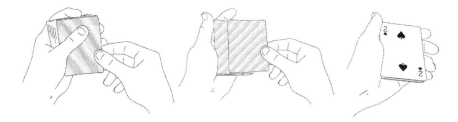

Do the same thing to turn them back over.

To make the flip back easier, you can flip them over the first time, so they hang over the bottom edge just a little. This makes it easier to grab them for the return flip.

Related Chapters:

- Breaks

BOTTOM SLIDE

The bottom slide allows you to place one card on the table while your spectator thinks it's another.

To do the bottom slide, start in a biddle grip.

Use your ring and pinky fingers to slide the bottom of the card out a little so you can take off the card above it.

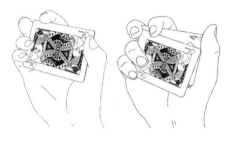

Use the same grip when dealing the cards off normally as well, so you do not have to change grip.

DROP REVEAL

In this reveal, you lift about half the deck off and then drop it back down. When it lands, your spectator's card will be face up on top.

Start with the cards in a mechanic's grip in your first hand. The card you want to reveal needs to be on top of the deck.

Bring your second hand over to pick up about half the deck using a biddle grip.

Just before you lift the cards up, use the thumb of your first hand to push the top card over about a third of the width of the cards. Use your second hand to conceal this action from the spectator.

Raise the cards about half a meter and then drop them onto a table, back onto the deck, or into your spectator's hand. The top card of the packet (your spectator's card) will flip over.

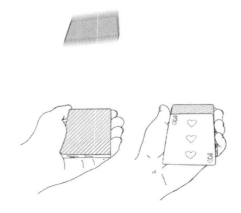

KEEPING TRACK
SEQUENCE

In this sequence, your spectator is asked to keep track of her cards, but is unable to do so because of your tricky finger work.

These tricks are also great to use individually as friendly "bar bets."

CIRCUS TRICK

Your spectator chooses a card and it gets shuffled back into the deck. You start dealing the cards face up and she sees her card getting dealt, but you keep going. A few cards later, you bet your spectator that the next card you flip over will be hers. Instead of flipping over the next card in the deck, you find your spectator's card in the pile you have already dealt and flip it over.

Method

Ask your spectator to choose a card and use the keycard method previously described to keep track of it.

When you cut the cards for the first time, do the cut below your spectator's card. Then when she cuts the cards, hopefully she will do it so her chosen card ends near the middle or top of the deck. This is not essential for the trick to work, but it makes it easier to present.

Start flipping cards face up on the table. Make it a bit messy.

When you see your keycard, you know her card will be the next selection. Place her card on the edge of the pile so it stays in sight while you continue to deal cards on top of it.

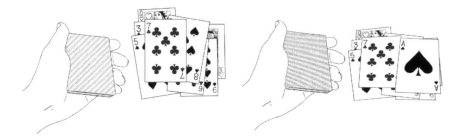

After five or so more cards, "bet" your spectator that the next card you flip over will be her selection. Instead of flipping over the next card, take her selection and flip it over face down.

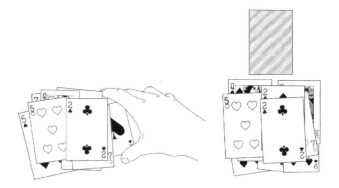

Related Chapters:

- Keycard

DR DALEY'S LAST TRICK

Four cards of a kind are selected from the deck. You show the two black cards to the spectator and place them in front of her. You then ask her to find the spade card.

When she chooses, she discovers she actually has the two red cards and you have the two black ones.

Method

Find all the cards with the value of your spectator's selection from the circus trick (four aces, in this example).

While you are doing this, tell her that it's now her turn to find her card.

Put the four cards in alternating colors, with her card (ace of spades) in the second position from the top. Don't draw attention to this. Do it while you are talking.

If you want, you can put a small bend in the cards to help with the double lift.

Show the front and back of the cards, two in each hand. Do it quickly, so your spectator doesn't take note of the position of her card.

As you close the spread, get a break under the top two cards.

Double-lift the two cards above your break to show your spectator her selection, then flip it back.

Flip the double back over and then put the top card (a red card, in this example) face down in front of her. Reiterate what she thinks it is by saying "I'll put the ace of spades in front of you."

Hold the cards on the top and bottom edge on one side with your thumb and middle finger.

Turn all three cards over to show the ace of clubs, then turn the cards back face down and then thumb off the top card.

Immediately after you thumb off the top card, flip the double over onto the card you thumbed off to show the ace of clubs.

Do this in one fluid motion.

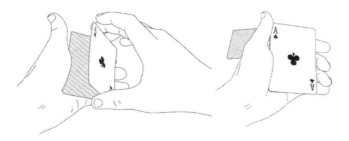

Double-lift the two cards back over, then take the top card and put it next to the first card in front of her. Reiterate what she thinks it is by saying "and here is the ace of clubs next to it." Put the other two cards face down on the table in front of you.

Ask your spectator to keep track of her card, then switch the position of the cards in front of her a few times, as if mixing them up.

Ask her to flip over her card. It will be wrong. Ask her to flip over the other one, which is also not hers. Reveal that the cards have switched.

Related Chapters:

- Double Lift
- Circus Trick

THREE-CARD MONTE

This is the classic three-card monte scam, in which you show three cards to the spectator and then place them face down on the table. She has to keep track of one of the cards while you mix them around.

Method

Tell your spectator that it's a bit hard to keep track when there are four cards, so this time you will only use three.

Get her selection (ace of spades) and the two cards of the opposite color (two red aces). Put an equal vertical bend in each of them. Do all three together—you do not want one to be different.

Grip with your thumb and middle finger as you pick each card up.

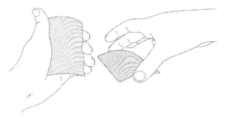

Show your spectator the three cards face up, then flip them all face down. Mix the three cards around in a simple manner so she can track her selection.

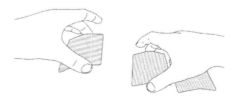

You can flash a card once or twice while you do it. Use smooth, flowing motions. Drop one card as you pick up another.

After your spectator successfully chooses her card, do the shuffle again. Make it a little faster, but still slow enough that the spectator should be able to get it.

The third time you do it, shuffle the cards around as normal, but keep track of your spectator's selection.

Once her selection is in the middle and you have picked up another card, pick up her card in the same hand, but with your ring finger and thumb.

The other card is still being held by your thumb and middle finger —this is the switch card.

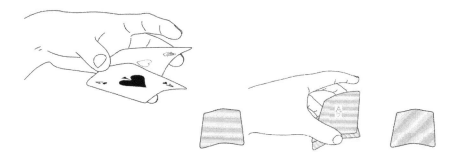

Flash her card to her, with the switch card behind it. As you go to set her selection card down, toss the switch card over instead.

Keep the flow going for a couple more turns, then ask your spectator to find her selection.

TRANSPORTING CARD

In this trick, your spectator's selection is placed on the bottom of the deck and the deck is split into three packets. You show her the bottom card of each packet and place each of the cards she sees, including her selection, in front of her.

When she is asked to find her card, she discovers it has disappeared. You then make it appear from the deck.

Method

Tell your spectator she can have one more chance to prove her observation skills.

Place whichever card you did not use in three-card monte (the one that isn't bent) on the bottom of the deck, then get your spectator to cut the deck into three equal piles.

Shuffle the packets around a little. Remember which one has her card in it.

Tell your spectator that you will show her the bottom card of each pile, and that she should mentally note which pile has her card in it. Show the bottom card of each pile to spectator and then place the bottom card face down in front of her.

When you get to the pile with her selection, use a bottom slide so you actually place down the card above her selection.

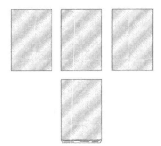

With the three cards on the table, collect the rest of them up. Ensure your spectator's card stays on the bottom, then use an overhand control to get it to the top. Place this packet aside.

Tell your spectator to keep track of her card, then mix the positions of the three cards on the table around a little. Get her to choose her card. It won't be there. Ask her to reveal the rest.

Use the drop reveal to produce your spectator's card from the deck.

Related Chapters:

- Bottom Slide
- Drop Reveal
- Three-Card Monte

SOULMATES

Learn several ways to "force" the spectator into choosing a specific card, as well as how to "control" his card so it appears in specific positions in the deck.

The accompanying four-trick sequence revolves around soulmate cards. Soulmate cards are two cards that share the same face value and color—the nine of spades and the nine of clubs, for example, or the king of hearts and the king of diamonds.

A soulmate opposite is the same card in the opposite color. For example, the opposite of a black nine is a red nine.

FORCES

A force is where the spectator thinks he is choosing a card freely, but he is really choosing the one you want him to choose.

Flip Force

The flip force is easy to perform and will fool most people. Start with the card you want the spectator to choose (the force card) on top of the deck.

Riffle the cards and have your spectator say "stop." Break the cards where he tells you to. Turn those cards face up and place them back onto the deck.

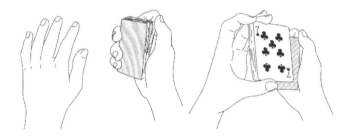

Riffle the cards again and have your spectator say "stop" again. Make sure he says stop after the face up cards. Break the cards where he tells you to. Turn those cards face up and place them back onto the deck.

Tell your spectator that his card will be the first card that is face down.

Slip Force

This force is a bit more slick than the flip force, and is just as easy to perform.

Have the card you want to force on top of the deck. Hold the deck in a mechanic's grip, but tilted on its side. The cards should face into your palm.

Use your thumb to riffle down the cards. Ask the spectator to say "stop" whenever he wants, and stop riffling when he does.

Bring your other hand over to pinch the cards on the short edges to pull them out. Keep pressure on the top card with your three fingers as you pull the rest of the cards out of the deck. This is the slip.

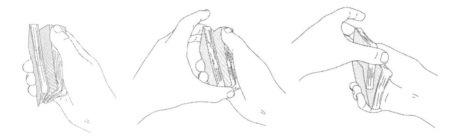

Immediately hit the edge of the cards you pulled out onto the remaining packet to square them up. This helps to cover the action of the slip.

Give your spectator the top card.

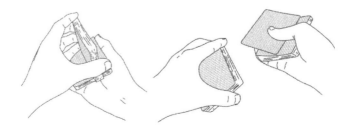

Spread Force

This is how you can force a card when using an in-hand spread for selection as opposed to a riffle.

Have the force card on top of the deck.

Peel the top card (the force card) off the deck and then spread the rest of the cards on top of it.

You can peel several cards off the top one at a time if you want; just make sure the force card is on the bottom of those peeled cards.

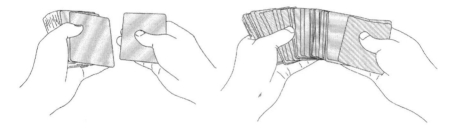

You need to keep a small gap between the force card and the spread.

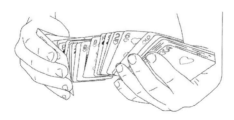

As you spread the cards out, have the spectator point to a card. Wherever he points, lift the cards up at that point and flick down on one with your thumb as you verbally confirm it is the one he wants.

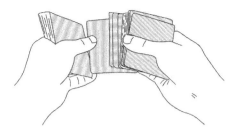

Use the cards from the packet in your left hand to square up the cards in your right hand, so that the force card ends on the bottom of that packet.

Show him the force card as his choice.

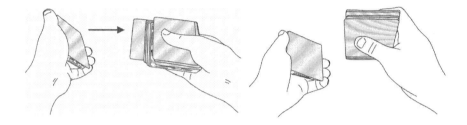

Related Chapters:

- In-Hand Spread

CONTROLS

A control is when you manipulate the chosen card(s) to move them to a specific place in the packet, usually the top or bottom.

Overhand Control

You can use the overhand shuffle for simple controls when you need to get the top card to the bottom or the bottom card to the top.

To control the top card to the bottom, first peel the top card off on its own, and then continue the rest of the shuffle on top of it.

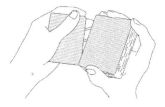

To control the bottom card to the top, do the overhand shuffle as normal, but make sure you finish it with the last card on the top.

Double Undercut

The double undercut is a way to move your spectator's card to the top or bottom of the deck.

Hold the deck in a mechanic's grip in your non-dominant hand. Grab about half the deck with your dominant hand and have your spectator place his card on top of the pile in your non-dominant hand.

Place the pile in your dominant hand on top of his card. As you do this, create a pinky break by jutting your little finger up so there is a small gap between the two piles of cards. Now you have a break in the cards above his card, but he can't see it from his view.

If he can see the break from the front, you have too much of your pinky between the cards.

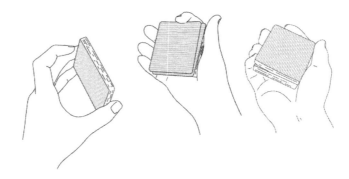

Shift the pinky break to a thumb break, then use your non-dominant hand to grab half the bottom packet and place it on top of the deck.

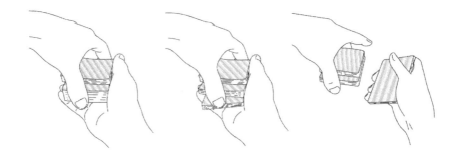

Do the same thing with the remainder of the bottom pile.

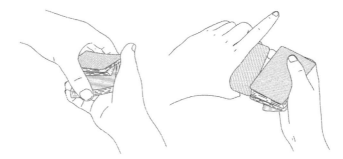

Now his card is on top. You can follow up with a false overhand and then a false riffle to keep it on top. If you need to move it to the bottom, using the overhand control instead of the false overhand.

The next two controls are variations of this basic double undercut.

Back-Push Control

Once you know the double undercut, the back-push control is easy to learn. Take the spectator's card and slide it into the deck from the back (the side closest to you).

Once it is halfway in, push it down and in to get the thumb break.

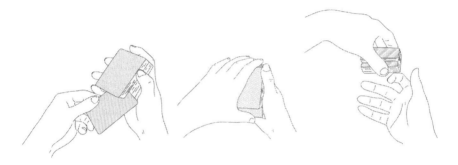

Do a double undercut to move it to the top.

To move your spectator's selection directly to the bottom, push it up and in so you get the break above the card below it.

Front-Push Control

This is similar to the back-push control but it comes in from the front, which means your spectator can place his card in the deck.

Ask the spectator insert his card about half a centimeter somewhere around the middle of the deck. The further he pushes it in, the harder it will be for you to perform the technique. If you are worried, you can put it in yourself.

Push the out-jogged card into the deck on a slight diagonal so the bottom of it comes out near your fingers.

Squeeze the card in square with your fingers so it becomes in-jogged.

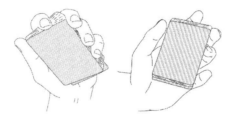

Move it to the top or bottom the same way as you would with the back-push control.

SOULMATES SEQUENCE

In this sequence, the spectator chooses a card and so do you. They are different, but after a little magic they turn into soulmates.

These two soulmate cards now find their respective soulmate opposites with a simple prediction trick.

Next, one of the four cards is mixed into the deck. Two other cards are then sent in to help find it.

The missing card is found, but now the two helper cards are lost in the deck. You throw the deck from one hand to the other and they appear.

CHANGING SOULMATES

Your spectator makes a selection and places the card face down on the table. You try to guess the soulmate of his card. You choose the wrong card, but place it on top of his selection anyway.

After a magical gesture, he looks at the card and it has changed into the soulmate of his selection.

Method

Peek at the top card and then force it to be your spectator's selection. Place the card face down on the table so neither of you see it.

Tell your spectator that you will now predict what the soulmate of his card is. Go through the cards and look for all the cards with the same face value as the force card. Don't let him see them.

Place the two soulmate opposites on the bottom and the soulmate to the top.

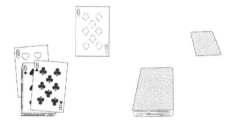

While you do this, explain what a soulmate card is. To cover why you are choosing several cards, say "maybe this one," "could be this one," etc.

When you are ready, ask your spectator to turn over his card. At the same time, do a double lift.

The card you predicted will be wrong. Double-lift it back, then place the top card (the real soulmate) face down on top of the force card (his selection), which is now faced up.

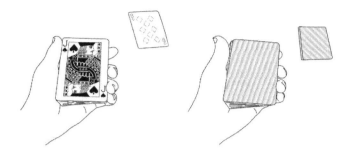

Say that your prediction skills are not good today, but perhaps your magic is better. Do something magical to the deck of cards (wave your hand over them, for example).

Get your spectator to look at the cards and see they are now soulmates.

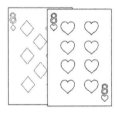

Related Chapters:

- Double Lift

PERFECT MATCH

Your spectator's soulmate cards will now find their soulmate Your spectator's soulmate cards will now find their soulmate opposites.

You deal cards face down on the table and wherever he says "stop," you place one of the original soulmates on the deck face up. This is done a second time. When the cards are spread out, it is revealed that the soulmate cards are directly next to their soulmate opposites.

Method

Tell your spectator that since your prediction skills were so bad last time, you will get him to predict this time.

As you say this, use a modified overhand control to get one of the two bottom cards (which are the soulmate opposites you positioned during the changing soulmates trick) from the bottom of the deck to the top, while also keeping one of them on the bottom.

To do this, pinch the deck between the thumb and fingers of your non-dominant hand while you pull out the cards.

Now you have two cards in your non-dominant hand, with the bottom card still on the bottom.

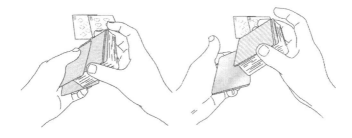

Do the overhand shuffle as normal but ensure that you peel the last card in your dominant hand off last as a single card.

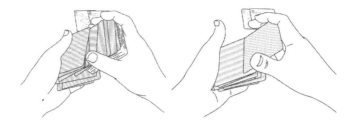

Now you have one of the soulmate opposites on the bottom of the deck and one on the top.

Deal cards on the table one at a time and ask your spectator to say "stop" whenever he wants.

Tell him you have a feeling the soulmate card is somewhere in the top half of the deck.

This isn't necessary for the trick to work, but it is better for presentation.

When he says "stop," pick up one of his soulmate cards and place it face up on top of the pile of cards you just dealt.

Place the rest of the deck on top. Do not let him see the bottom card.

Start dealing the cards again, the same way as before. Ask him to stay "stop" when he feels like it. Tell him you have a feeling the second soulmate card is before the first face-up card.

When he says "stop," place his other soulmate card face up on top of the pile.

Place the remaining cards on top.

Reveal that he has successfully placed his cards on top of their soul-mate opposites.

Related Chapters:

- Changing Soulmates

HELPING HAND

Your spectator selects one of his four cards and it is mixed into the deck. The two soulmate opposites are placed into the middle of the deck. As they are pushed in, another card protrudes out the other end. Amazingly, it is his selection.

Method

Ask you spectator to choose any one of his four cards. Whichever he chooses, place it in the deck and move it to the top using a control.

Tell him to give you the two soulmate opposites of the card he just gave you. Explain that these are the helper cards which will go into the deck to find the missing one.

As he picks up the cards to hand them to you, get a pinky break on the top card of the deck, which is his card.

Take the two helper cards and place them face down on top of the deck. Now you have three cards on top of your break.

Square the cards up and then lift all three of the top cards. Thumb off the very top card, so it is out-jogged on top of the deck.

Turn the cards over to show it to the spectator.

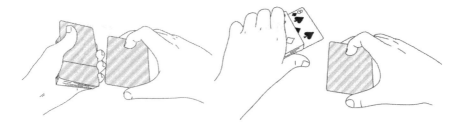

Place the remaining two cards (which he thinks is one) on top of the deck, but not out-jogged.

Use your index finger to slide out the top card so it is past the first out-jogged card. Make sure you keep the cards square so it looks like there is nothing in between the two out-jogged cards.

Show your spectator both cards.

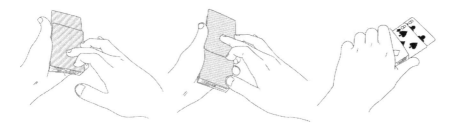

Turn them back face down and push the two out-jogged cards flush with each other.

Explain to your spectator that you will now send them into to the deck to find the missing card. Take about half the cards off the bottom of the deck and place them on top of the out-jogged cards.

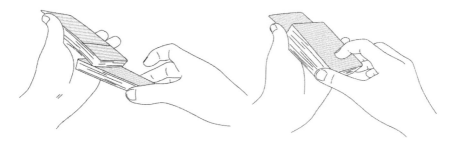

Turn the cards around 180 degrees, so the out-jogged cards are pointing towards you. Now they are in-jogged.

Say that the two soulmate opposites need a little help from the missing card's soulmate card. Get the spectator to pick up the soulmate of the missing card and give the deck a little tap with it.

Push the in-jogged cards into the deck, but not all the way in. This will push his card out the other side. It is important not to push them all the way in so you can flow into the last trick of this sequence.

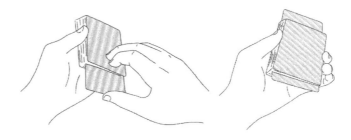

Rotate his card horizontally in the tip of the deck. Give it a flick down and it will land on the table face up.

PLAYING CATCH

The helper cards did their job, but now they are missing in the deck.

As a final trick, you throw the cards from one hand to the other, and the missing soulmate pair is extracted from the deck.

Method

To extract the two missing cards, you will do the pinch throw, which is a type of reveal that creates the illusion of you plucking two cards from random spots in the deck.

Tell your spectator that now all that is left to do is to rescue the two cards missing in the deck.

As you are talking, use a back-push control to move the two opposite soulmate cards to the bottom of the deck.

Follow up with the modified overhand control (as explained in the perfect match trick) so you have one of his cards on the bottom of the deck and one on top.

Ensure the cards are squared off and pinch them in one hand. Your thumb should be on top and your other four fingers should be on the bottom.

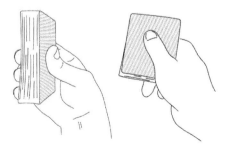

Once you have the cards in position, get your spectator to get the two cards he has and tap the deck with them twice.

Do a couple of waves, gradually getting faster.

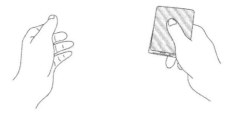

Throw the deck from one hand to the other. As you throw the cards, keep a loose pinch on the top and bottom ones so they end up being the only cards left in your hand.

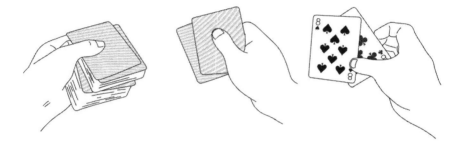

Related Chapters:

- Perfect Match

REVERSALS

Learn ways to secretly reverse cards in the deck, as well as how to
fake count and steal cards so the spectator thinks you have more or
less than you actually do.

CARD STEAL/FAKE COUNTING

This is a method of counting out cards in front of your spectator where you take a card back without her knowing. Use this to make your spectator think there are more cards than there actually are, and/or to steal back a specific card.

You can do this with a full deck, but it is easier to practice with a smaller packet first.

Hold the packet of cards in your dominant hand in a straddle grip. Use the thumb of your other hand to slide the top card off into a mechanic's grip.

Get a pinky break underneath whichever card you want to steal back.

As you slide off the next card, slip the card you have the pinky break under back into your hand. The card you stole is now on the bottom of the packet in your dominant hand

If there is no specific card you need to steal back, just steal back the first one and then continue to count them off as normal. You will end up counting off one more card than you actually have.

With practice you can count off more cards, but don't go too far—otherwise, it will be obvious that the packet is too thin for the number of cards you are supposed to have.

REVERSALS SEQUENCE

This sequence highlights ways of getting your spectator's card to appear in reverse position from the rest of the cards in the deck.

BIDDLE TRICK

Your spectator selects a card. You try to read her mind and select several cards that you think it could be. You show the cards to your spectator and she sees her card, but doesn't tell you. The cards are placed in her hand. When you make a magical gesture, her card vanishes and reappears upside down in the deck.

Method

Peek at the top card and force it onto your spectator. Let her shuffle the cards. In this example, the force card is the queen of spades

Tell your spectator that you are going to try to read her mind to find out what her card was. Look thoughtfully into her eyes as you go through the cards, out-jogging cards that you think it might be. Use patter such as "I have a strong feeling it's a black card," "maybe a high number," etc.

Out-jog five cards in total. Ensure her selection is the second one you out-jog, and make all the other cards the same color and of similar face value.

Square up and strip out the cards you chose. Turn the rest of the deck face down while the five selections stay face up.

Tell your spectator that you are pretty sure one of your selections is her card, but you are not sure exactly which one, so you need a little more help.

Cut the bottom half of the deck onto the table. Strip off the five selections into your other hand as you say the value of each one.

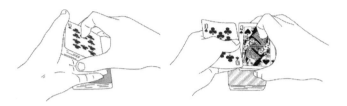

As you strip off the second card (her selection), hold a break under it.

As you strip the third one, take back the second one (her selection) using the card steal.

Keep the four cards in your hand and place the remainder of the packet on top of the rest of the deck. Turn over the four remaining cards and do a fake count to count four cards as five.

Place the four cards face down on the table (or in your spectator's hand). Ask your spectator to concentrate on her card. Predict what her card is (say the force card).

Tell your spectator that now that you know her card, you can transport it back into the deck. Bring the deck face up over the four cards (which are face down) on the table (or in her hands) and wave it over them.

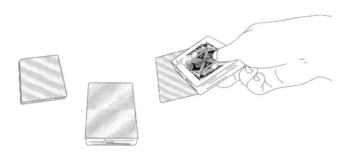

Ask your spectator to give her selected card back to you. She will discover it is missing. Reveal that you have transported it, and it is now upside down in the deck.

Related Chapters:

- Out-jogging
- Card Steal/Fake Counting

BRAUE REVERSAL

Your spectator's card is placed back in the deck and shuffled in, only for her to discover it has reversed itself again.

Method

Shuffle your spectator's card back into the deck and move it to the top using a control. Get a pinky break on the top card (her selection), then shift it to a thumb break. Tell your spectator that now you know her card, it is easy for you to make it reverse itself.

Undercut half the deck and put it on top of the break card, face up. Now you have about half a deck of face-up cards, one face-down card (her selection), a break, then the rest of the cards, face down.

Immediately undercut all the cards under the break and show them directly to your spectator. Put the two halves back together so that her selection is in the middle and the only one reversed.

Tell your spectator that now all the cards are upside down, but all you need to do is give the deck a little shake.

Shake the cards, then turn the whole deck face down. Reveal that her card is once again the only one upside down.

TRIUMPH

Once again the card is placed back in the deck and shuffled in. As an extra shuffle, you also turn about half the cards upside down. Amazingly, all the cards turn back to facing the same way, except one—her selection.

Method

Shuffle your spectator's card back into the deck and control it to the bottom. With the cards in a biddle grip, secretly bend them a little.

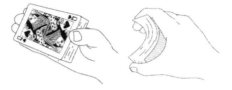

Tell your spectator that this time, you are going to make things a little harder by mixing the cards face up and down.

While holding the deck in a mechanic's grip, take five to ten cards. Turn them over and place them on top of the deck.

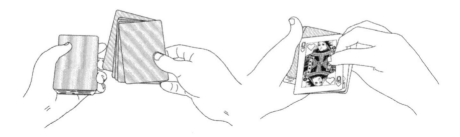

Do it again with the next five to ten cards. Work through the whole deck in this flip-flop manner.

Once you get to the bottom, flip the cards over and put your spectator's card face down on top.

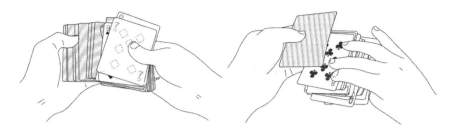

If you have done it right, you will have half the cards face down and half face up, except for your spectator's card, on top. Don't show her this.

Prove to your spectator that the cards are all mixed up by splitting them about a third of the way down to show them face-to-back.

Split them three quarters of the way down as well, to show them back-to-face.

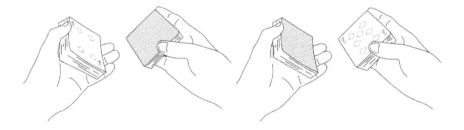

There will be a natural gap in the middle of the deck from the bend you put in the cards. Split the cards there to show cards back-to-back.

When you return them, flip the top portion over.

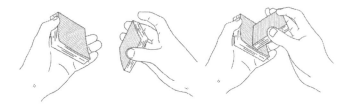

Now all the cards except hers are facing one way.

Shake the cards a little, then wait and do it again. Do this several times. Tell your spectator that since the cards are very mixed up, it will take a few more shakes.

Reveal that all the cards are face down except for her selection.

AMBITIOUS CARD

Add the marlo tilt and the turnover pass to your repertoire of card-handling skills, then learn one of the most famous card sequences ever performed—the Ambitious Card trick.

TURNOVER PASS

A pass is a type of control where the spectator can't see what you are doing, as opposed to a double undercut, where he sees the cards move.

There are many types of passes, and in general they are intermediate to advanced techniques, except for this one.

In this case, angle yourself a little to the side of your spectator to get the best position. Spread the cards out face up.

Have your spectator touch or name a card he sees. Place your pinky under it so you can get a break as you square up the cards.

You need to rotate both packets from face up to face down at the same time, but as separate packets.

To do this, take off the top packet and dip the hand holding the bottom packet, so the cards end up on their edges in your hand.

The two packets should make a T. Dip both hands down a little as you do this.

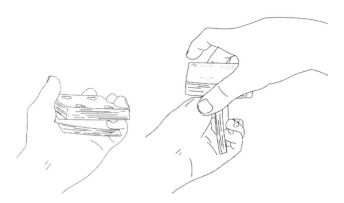

As you bring your hands back up, use your index finger to turn over the top packet, and then place it on top of the bottom packet.

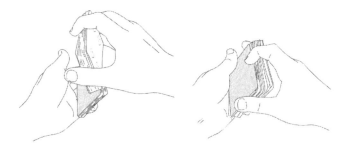

Perform these two actions so the packets are as close as possible together without touching as they turn. The down-up action helps conceal the pass.

Use the fingertips of your bottom hand to push the bottom packet up, so the deck ends up flat, as it started. Square of the deck to re-establish your mechanic's grip.

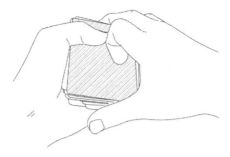

It is best not to shuffle the cards after doing a pass, because your spectator already thinks his selection is in the middle of the deck.

MARLO TILT

The marlo tilt is a way for you to move a card to the second position from the top. It makes use of an optical illusion, as opposed to the false shuffles of other controls, to fool the spectator.

To do the marlo tilt, get a large pinky break on the top card. You want the break to be the whole width of the card, as opposed to just the corner.

Although there is a big gap in the back, you still want it to look normal from the front. Don't let your spectator see the side.

You will be placing the card into the deck from behind, but first, use the corner of the card to push a few cards in the middle of the deck so they out-jog a little. This helps create the effect that you are putting the selected card in the middle.

After a few taps, slide the card into the gap created by your break. Square the deck up.

Related Chapters:

- False Shuffles
- Controls

MAGICIAN'S CHOICE

Magician's choice is a type of force where the spectator thinks he is choosing from multiple options, but in reality you are guiding his final choice to be the one you want. It is often used as a reveal.

A simple version is when you have card A and card B, and card A is the one you want him to choose. Ask him to point to one of the cards.

If he points to card A, tell him that it is his choice and discard card B.

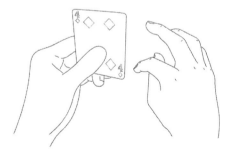

If he points to card B, tell him that card is the one to discard, leaving him with card A as his selection.

Expanding this to three cards (A, B, and C) is similar. Ask him to select two options. If he chooses A and another card, discard the leftover card, then do it again with two cards as previously described.

If his first choice is B and C, discard them both, so A becomes his selection.

You can expand this further to more cards. It gets harder to track, but the principle remains the same. You just need to remember where the force card is. If there are many cards, you can bring it down to two or three choices by asking him to pick from piles of cards to begin with, and then narrow it down to single cards.

AMBITIOUS CARD SEQUENCE

Ambitious Card is a classic sequence where a card is selected and returned to the middle of the pack. Something magical is done and it jumps to the top. This happens several times, each time being more impressive than the last.

There are many ways to do this sequence. You can add, subtract, and move tricks around to create your own version.

BROKEN ELEVATOR

This Ambitious Card sequence starts off with a bit of a warm-up, where the card does not make it all the way to the top.

Method

Ask your spectator to select any card and move it to the top using the turnover pass. In this example, the selected card is the ace of diamonds.

Explain that this card is connected to the spectator, and that he should be able to bring it to the top with just a click of his fingers. Get your spectator to click his fingers, then do a double lift to reveal it is not his card.

Feign disappointment, saying that sometimes the card doesn't make it all the way to the top the first time, but that it should have made it into the top portion of the deck. Ask him to choose a number between 5 and 15.

Whatever number he chooses (position X), deal that number of cards on the table as a demonstration of what you need him to do.

His card is now on the bottom of the packet on the table. Pick up that packet and place it on the rest of the deck. Now his card is in position X.

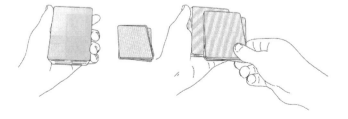

Give your spectator the cards to deal and explain that he needs to deal the same number of cards onto the table as you did, because it will only work for him, since he is the one connected to the card.

Once he has finished dealing, ask him to pick up the last card he dealt and place it on his hand.

Get him to click his fingers over the card, then to flip it over.

Related Chapters:

- Double Lift
- Turnover Pass

CARD CALL

In this trick, your spectator's card is placed back into the deck, then instantly appears on top again when he snaps his fingers.

Method

As your spectator is doing the click and turn from the reveal of Broken Elevator, shuffle the rest of the cards into the deck and get a big break on the top card as you square them up.

Get your spectator's card and place it in the deck using the marlo tilt.

Explain that the card should make it to the top this time. Have your spectator snap his fingers. Do a double lift to show the card made it.

Related Chapters:

- Double Lift
- Marlo Tilt

JUMPING CARD

In this sequence, the spectator's card is placed in the deck again, but this time, half the cards are put aside to make it easier for the card to find its way to the top.

His card is summoned to the top of the packet that is remaining, but doesn't make it. It is then revealed that the card actually went to the top of the other packet, which you put aside.

Method

Double-lift the cards back over from the card-call trick. Explain that this time, you will make it a bit harder. Take off the top card, which he thinks is his card, and then ask him to take the top half of the deck. Place "his card" in your half of the deck.

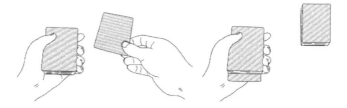

Ask your spectator to snap his fingers. Turn over the top card of the packet in your hand—it will be wrong. Explain to him that it's because the you don't have the top of the deck—he does. Ask him to turn over the top card in his packet to reveal that the card has jumped over.

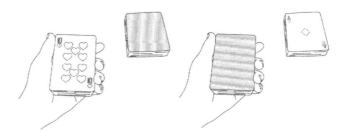

CARD POP

For this trick in this sequence, you bend the spectator's selection and place it in the deck. He snaps his fingers and the card visibly pops up to the top.

Method

Put the deck back together except for your spectator's card. Tell him that this time, you will make it harder still by shuffling the deck after you have put the card in.

Put his card in the deck and control it to the top. Use a riffle shuffle to get it to the second position from the top.

Ask your spectator to snap his fingers. Do a double lift to show the card made it.

Lift up the two cards in a biddle grip and show your spectator the face value of his card. Explain that this time, he will get to see the card rise to the top.

Bend the cards enough so there is a visible curve, but don't put a crease in them.

Place both cards on the top of the deck, then cut the deck. Place your finger on top of the two bent cards so they don't split.

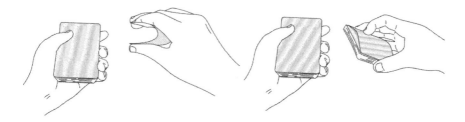

Peel off the top bent card onto the second packet and use your index finger to press down on the other bent card (his selection) so it looks flat.

Raise the packet with the second card up a little to draw attention and so he can clearly see it is bent.

Place the top packet on top of the bent card and hold the deck in your thumb and fingers along the side. Make sure your fingers hold the top card down flat.

Tell your spectator that you want him to snap his fingers on the count of three. When he does, release the tension from your thumb and fingers to allow the top card to pop up.

Flip it over to reveal his card.

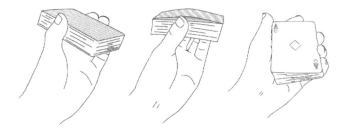

Related Chapters:

- Shuffling
- Double Lift

APPEARING CARD

In this sequence, your spectator's card gets shuffled back into the deck. You show him three random cards that are not his selection and place them on the table. He clicks his fingers over each of them, then chooses one of the cards. It is his selection.

Method

Take the spectator's card, straighten it out, then move it to the bottom of the deck using a control.

You now need to move it to the fourth position from the bottom. Do this with a riffle shuffle by allowing three cards to fall from one portion of the deck before letting his card go from the other portion.

Alternatively, get a pinky break on the top three cards and move them to the bottom with a double undercut.

As you are doing the card straightening and control, tell your spectator that this time you are really going to test his connection with the card. Say that you will show him three cards, and place them in front of him. Explain that the chances of him seeing his card are very slim, since it has been shuffled into the deck, but if he does see his card, to let you know.

Show your spectator the bottom card, then place it face down on the table. Next, move the new bottom card to the top of the deck.

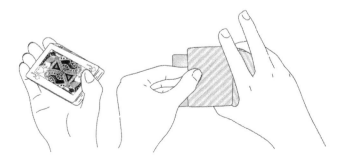

Show him the next card, then use a bottom slide and place his selected card face down on the table. Move the real bottom card to the top of the deck.

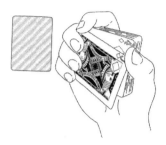

For the third card, do it normally, like you did the first time. Show your spectator the card, place it down, then move the next one to the top. Place the deck to the side.

Ask your spectator if he saw his card. He will say no. Get him to click his fingers over each of the cards one time.

Use the magician's choice to force your spectator to choose his card, which is the one in the middle.

Related Chapters:

- Bottom Slide
- Magician's Choice

COLOR CHANGES

Color changes are when a card instantly changes from one to another.

This section also explains how to create a vanishing card effect. While it is not technically a color change, it does make the card instantly disappear.

PALMING

Palming is when you conceal an object in your hand. There are a few different methods for palming. Here are some that you can use with cards and other small objects.

When palming cards, remember to use a light touch and pay close attention to your angles.

Classic Palm

The classic palm is when the card is held between your pinky and the base of your thumb. The rest of your fingers might touch the card, but they don't apply any pressure.

Don't stick your thumb out or leave gaps between your fingers. Keeping your fingertips touching will prevent these gaps.

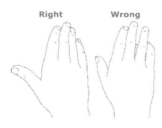

Ideally, you want the width of your hand to be greater than the width of the card, but it is still possible to perform this move if your hands are smaller. Allow the card to stick out beyond your pinky a little and tilt your hand to conceal it.

To get the top card into the classic palm, first out-jog it a little. Lightly press on the top right corner of the card with your pinky to pop the card into your hand. While doing this, hold the cards on a diagonal to prevent flashing.

Once you have a card in the classic palm, you need to position your hands in a natural way while not flashing. Ensure the back of the hand the card is held in faces your spectator while you hold something or hand him the cards.

If you want to bring your hand down, don't drop it straight down, as that is too obvious. Instead, simultaneously bring the deck higher and your palmed card lower. Your hand needs to drop naturally.

Gambler's Palm

In the gambler's palm, the card is held between the little finger and the fleshy part of the side of the thumb. It is held lower down than in the classic palm and on a different angle.

Tenkai Palm

The tenkai palm is a sleight of hand you can use to make many different small objects disappear.

Hold the card between your index and middle fingers at around the middle of the short end of the card.

Curl the card in with your fingers.

Bring your thumb over to hold the card in your palm and then extend your fingers. Keep your thumb low throughout the sleight so it doesn't suddenly disappear.

To present this sleight, you can use a throwing motion. Do a couple out-in actions first, then, on the last one, make the card disappear. As the card disappears, look to where you are "throwing" the card. This helps to misdirect your spectator's attention, as people will naturally look to where you look.

Alternatively, use a grabbing motion with your other hand so it is like you are scrunching the card up, then reveal that the scrunching hand is empty. Your hand provides cover while you do the tenkai palm.

COLOR CHANGES

There are many different ways to do color changes. Here are four to start you off. They are not in a "flowing sequence" like the tricks in previous section, but they do go in order of ease to perform—though those you actually find easier to perform may differ from the order they are given in here.

SHAKE CHANGE

In this move, your spectator chooses a random card from the deck and it gets shuffled back into the pack. You choose a card and show it to her, asking "is this your card?" Your selection is incorrect. You then shake the card and it magically changes into the spectator's card.

Method

Let your spectator choose a card, then move it to the top with a control.

Tell your spectator you will now find her card. Fan through the deck face down and out-jog a random card. As you square up the deck, get a pinky break under the top card (her selection).

Pull out the random out-jogged card and place it face up on top of your break. Now her card and the wrong card are back-to-back.

Square the two cards together and ask her if you got her card. She will say no. Feign disappointment, saying that your prediction skills have never been very good, but luckily you know some magic.

Double-lift the cards by placing your middle finger on the top right of them and your thumb on the bottom left. Hold the cards as flat as possible while still being able to reach the top edge with your index finger. You may need to bend the corners of the cards down a little with your thumb and middle finger so the middle pops up.

Slowly wave your from hand side to side. When you are ready, increase your speed and use your index finger to flip the cards over. Do this by placing your index finger on the top edge of the card, close to your middle finger, and curling it in towards you. The finger curl won't completely turn the card, so you will need to turn your hand a little as you perform it.

Tip: Practice the finger curl on its own before you try it with the wave.

Once the card has "changed," put them both on top of the deck. Give your spectator the top card to inspect and give the deck quick cut to mix in the top card.

DROP CHANGE

In this trick, your spectator chooses a card and it gets shuffled back into the deck. She then tries to guess where her card is in the deck. She chooses the wrong card but then you magically change it into her selection.

Your spectator's card is placed into the deck then instantly jumps back to the top.

Method

Let your spectator choose a card, then move it to the bottom with a control. In this example, the chosen card is the ten of spades.

Tell your spectator that she is now going to try predict where her card is in the deck. Fan the cards out, face down, and ask her to touch the card she feels might be hers.

Place the card on the table and then square the rest of the deck up. As you square the cards back up, get a pinky break on the bottom card (her selection).

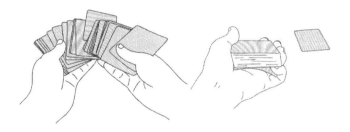

Ask your spectator how confident she is that she chose her card. Her answer doesn't matter. Tell her to look at the card to see if she got it right.

As she looks at it, use your fingers to flip over her real selection (which is on the bottom of the deck). Maintain the pinky break.

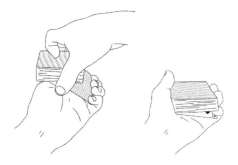

Tell your spectator not to worry about not guessing the card right, because there is something else you can do to find it. Have her place the wrong card face up on the deck.

Grab the deck with your other hand in a biddle grip as you shift the pinky break to a thumb break, then swing-cut the top half of the deck back into your other hand.

Cover the face-up card she guessed with the cards in your biddle grip. Drop her card on top, push it up, then bring the top packet away.

Bring the bottom pile to the top, then use a double lift to turn over both the cards facing down.Grab the top card and push it into the middle of the pack.

Ask your spectator to click her fingers, then reveal that her selection has jumped back to the top of the deck.

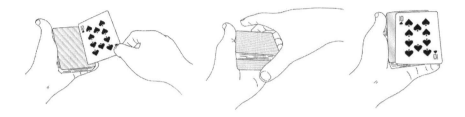

Related Chapters:

- Double Lift

STILETTO CHANGE

In this trick, your spectator chooses a card and it gets shuffled back into the deck. You pick up the top card and show the spectator that it isn't her card. You then smack it against the deck, and it changes into her original selection right before her eyes.

Method

Let your spectator choose a card, then move it to the top with a control. You are going to do a double lift with a little flourish in order to get your hand in the correct position for the color change.

Get a pinky break under the top two cards, then pick them up as a double by their diagonally opposite corners. Your middle finger should be on the top right corner and your thumb should be on the bottom left corner.

Lift it up to show it to your spectator. You can bend the cards a little to prevent them slipping apart.

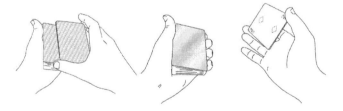

Place your index finger in the middle of the top edge, then curl it in and extend it back out, so that the cards spin on their corners.

Bring your index finger back to spin the cards back the other way, then grip the cards on the bottom edge with your middle finger.

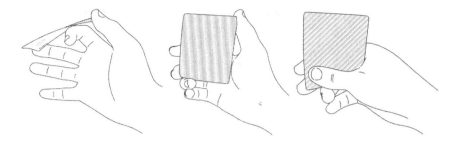

Bring the deck and the cards together so they meet vertically in a "slap." Just before they connect, slide the front card down. The slap will also mask the sound of the slide. Pull the deck away so you are left with only your spectator's selection in your hand. The front card should stay on the deck.

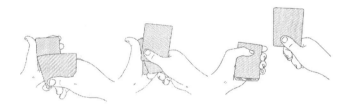

Hand your spectator the card for inspection as you shuffle the other card into the deck.

Front view.

CARDINI CHANGE

In this trick, your spectator chooses a card and you shuffle it back into the deck. She is shown a random card and holds it between her hands. She is then shown another random card.

After quick wave from the magician (you), the second random card magically changes into the first random card.

The spectator then looks in her hands to find she is holding her original selection.

Method

Fan the cards out face up and ask her to point to any card. Do a turnover pass to move that card it to the top. In this example, the chosen card is the ten of clubs.

Confirm what her choice was and then say that now you will choose a card. Do a double lift. Whatever the card is will be your selection. In this example, your selection is the two of diamonds.

Reiterate what her card is, as well as what your card is. Flip the double back over, then give your spectator the top card (her card), saying, "I'll give you my card." Make sure she doesn't look at it. A good way to do this is to place it face down in her hand and immediately get her to cover it with her other hand. Alternatively, just put it face down on the table in front of her and say "I'll put my card over here, out of the way."

Do another double lift and ask if the card you come up with is hers. She will say no. Tell her you are going to make her card appear. This is where you do the cardini change.

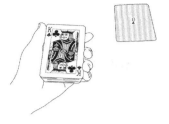

Assuming the cards are in a mechanic's grip in your non-dominant hand, angle yourself so your non-dominant shoulder is a bit closer to your spectator. Tilt the cards down a little, away from the spectator's eye-line.

As you are positioning yourself, bring your dominant hand over to square up the cards. As you do so, change the grip in your non-dominant hand so that you are holding the deck high in your hand with your thumb and index fingertips. This will give you enough room to do the sleight.

Wave your dominant hand over the deck. Do it close to the top of the deck so it provides the right cover.

As your waving hand comes back towards you, use the pinky of your non-dominant hand to drag the top card down diagonally over the bottom corner of the second card.

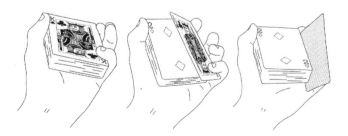

Grab the deck in a straddle grip with your dominant hand as you use the fingers of your non-dominant hand to drag the card underneath the deck.

The drag will leave your non-dominant hand in an unnatural position. To cover it, use your dominant hand to rotate them clockwise. Make a 180 degree rotation and then place them back in your non-dominant hand.

After doing the change, look surprised and say "Oh, I've accidentally changed it to my card instead of yours. So what have you got then?"

Get your spectator to look at the card you placed on the table (or in her hands) to discover it is her original selection.

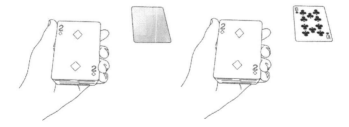

Related Chapters:

- Double Lift
- Turnover Pass

VANISHING CARD

In this trick, a single card vanishes right before the spectator's eyes. Both of the magician's hands are shown to be empty. The card then magically reappears.

Method

Hold a single card in your hand between your fingers and start to bring your other hand over. Do the tenkai palm with a grab motion to make it look like you are scrunching the card up.

You need to be very careful with your spectator's line of sight throughout this whole effect.

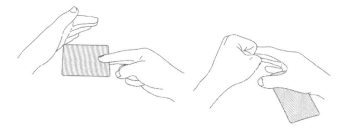

Show the hand you scrunched the card up with to be empty.

Drop the card into the gambler's palm, which is at the bottom end of your palm. Continue to bring your hand forward and turn it over to show it empty.

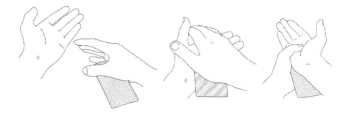

Turn your hand back over and palm the card so you can show the other hand to be empty.

To make the card reappear, keep it palmed as you pull it out with your other hand.

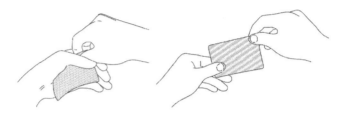

THANKS FOR READING

Dear reader,

Thank you for reading *Basic Card Magic*.

If you enjoyed this book, please leave a review where you bought it. It helps more than most people think.

Don't forget your FREE book chapters!

You will also be among the first to know of FREE review copies, discount offers, bonus content, and more.

Go to:

https://offers.SFNonfictionBooks.com/Free-Chapters

Thanks again for your support.

AUTHOR RECOMMENDATIONS

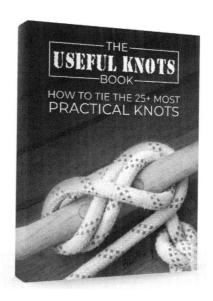

Discover the Only Knots You'll Ever Need

Teach yourself knot tying today, because it's easy, fun, and useful.

Get it now.

www.SFNonfictionbooks.com/Useful-Knots-Book

Teach Yourself Escape and Evasion Tactics

Discover the skills you need to evade and escape capture, because you never know when they will save your life.

Get it now.

www.SFNonfictionBooks.com/Evading-Escaping-Capture

ABOUT SAM FURY

Sam Fury has had a passion for survival, evasion, resistance, and escape (SERE) training since he was a young boy growing up in Australia.

This led him to years of training and career experience in related subjects, including martial arts, military training, survival skills, outdoor sports, and sustainable living.

These days, Sam spends his time refining existing skills, gaining new skills, and sharing what he learns via the Survival Fitness Plan website.

www.SurvivalFitnessPlan.com

amazon.com/author/samfury

goodreads.com/SamFury

facebook.com/AuthorSamFury

instagram.com/AuthorSamFury

youtube.com/SurvivalFitnessPlan

Printed in Great Britain
by Amazon

85204294R10086